D1251367

AN UNFORGETTABLE JOURNEY

An Unforgettable Journey: Pushing to the Finish

Copyright © 2021 Overseer Angela Coleman

This manuscript has undergone viable editorial work and proofreading, yet human limitations may have resulted in minor grammatical or syntax-related errors remaining in the finished book. The understanding of the reader is requested in these cases.

This book is set in the typeface *Athelas* designed by Veronika Burian and Jose Scaglione.

Paperback ISBN: 9798487826404

A Publication of *Tall Pine Books | tallpinebooks.com*

*Published in the United States of America

AN UNFORGETTABLE JOURNEY

PUSHING TO THE FINISH

ANGELA COLEMAN

DEDICATION &
ACKNOWLEDGEMENTS

To my Papa, my (Abba) Father God, thank you for the life of your Word that continues to keep me daily. It is because of You, Your promises to me, and Your covenant with me, that I continue this race.

Upon writing this publication there were so many mixed emotions that I experienced as I progressed from one chapter to the next.

It brought back numerous memories of my journey with my lifetime best friend and partner on this earth. I never expected him not seeing the printed pages.

I dedicate this book in memory of my late husband, Bishop Allen B. Coleman. Thank you for your uncompromising Yes to the Lord, as it plowed the way for my Yes!

To our daughters, Erica, and Charity. You both sacrificed so much over the many years joining Momma and Daddy on the ministry trail. Thank you for hanging in there. I love you both!

To my "Aaron and Hur", Pastor Vanilla Pittman and Pastor Andrea Selby. Thank you both for continuing to lift my arms as God's strength prevails through us. I am eternally grateful for your tenacity to push along with me and continue a life of legacy! Its to the Finish!

Thanks also to my (Son in Love), Andrew Adam III and grandchildren, Andrew IV, Angela, Allen and Amarissa for all your prayers and support. Nana loves you all!

Thank you "V.O. J." family! We are not just a name we are a mantle! Let's continue to be a House of God's Glory!

CONTENTS

1

MY BEGINNING

(A CINDERELLA STORY)

The year was 1978. After finishing high school, I went to live with my mother on the eastside of town. She was caring for my Great Grandmother, Eola Green, who was in her 80's at that time. She was a very sweet and wise woman who didn't say much but, at times you would catch her smiling. When I had the opportunity, I would sit with her and just let her talk. I'm so glad I had a chance to spend time with her before she transitioned.

It was a little different for me at first being in unfamiliar territory, but I was happy to be back with my mother after such a long time. After getting adjusted with her and my Great Grandmother, I begin to fit in somewhat. The Eastside was where my mother's family grew up. Believe me, it wasn't Ponte Vedra.

Now that I had graduated and was living with my mother again, I had to find something else to do. I began looking for a summer job. I applied and was hired at NAS JAX. I was very excited to have a summer job and making very good money. I didn't have any bills or other responsibilities at that time, so I spent my money on others, especially at Christmas time.

When the summer was over, I had a lot of time on my hands and needed something else to do. I had a family member that worked at the Downtown Hilton Hotel where some of my other family members worked, and she asked if I was interested in having a job there with them. After taking the job, I had another cousin who I became very close with, and we worked together on many assignments. As we would go into work, we would notice many of the workers moving about on their daily routines. On one of those days, we came across two brothers who were having Bible study during their lunch break. We had no idea what we were in for!

We were two nosey girls snooping around to see what was going on, which turned out to be the best thing that ever happened to me. After meeting the two brothers we noticed they were different. There was something about them that you didn't ordinarily see with guys when it came to flirting with the girls. We asked them, "do you all dance? They said, "not the kind of dancing you think!" We began to badger them with other worldly questions. That's when one of them said, "Will you all attend our Bible study on one of our lunch breaks?" At first, we were hesitant, but curious, so we began attending the Bible studies and started being convicted.

You see for me, many years ago before I moved with my mother, I attended a CME Church, but I didn't have any understanding of what it meant to be saved. I was in the choir and gave my penny offering when I was asked. During that time, pennies were easy to come by. I also didn't know what it meant to tithe.

Back to the two brothers, they began to draw us in a little more as we attended more of the Bible studies. For me, the more Bible studies I attended the more I was convicted by the Word. I realized it wasn't about the physical attraction of the brothers, but it was about my need for God. Something started happening on the inside of me to want to know more about who God was and this thing about being saved. The younger brother, Allen, said to me, "If you have any more questions, I will give you my number and you can call me, and I will explain what's happening to you."

I agreed to take his number and I decided to call him. He began to share St. John 3:16 with me in detail. All I could do was cry on the phone. There was a noticeable breaking in me. That opened the door for him to lead me in the sinner's prayer. Hallelujah for that! He had me to repeat the prayer after him to receive Jesus as my Lord and Savior. Oh, what a day that was for me! It changed my life forever! After leading me into the sinner's prayer, he said to me now go and tell someone what happened to you. The first person I saw was my Great Grandmother.

She looked at me and gave me the biggest smile and said, "that's good, I'm happy for you." I don't know what I was feeling at the time. The best way I knew to explain it was to acknowledge that I had done something good. But what about the things of my past and the relationships? How am I going to explain my new life decision? The next person I told was my mother. I thought she would be excited about my new decision for Christ, but her response was, "you're too young to do that!"

It became very difficult for me in my relationship with my mother at first until she finally accepted my decision. In my new life with Christ, the first thing that changed was my appetite for the music I used to listen to. Then, I had to confront old friends to let them know I wasn't the same person. It wasn't easy, but it was necessary. I was willing to let go of the old so that I could embrace the new and to this day, I do not regret one moment of the decision I made. New life, new start!

2

THE PROPOSAL

Soon after the Lord used my husband to lead me into the sinner's prayer and I received the Lord as my Savior, he invited me to his Church to a Service they were having. He didn't own a car at the time, so someone had to pick us up for the Service. He was very serious about attending church and any other ministry opportunities that were available. After attending the Service, out of nowhere, he asked me if I would like to go home or to go by his home.

In my thoughts, I wondered why he would ask me that question. This is a person I really did not know very well, and I wasn't feeling totally comfortable with him yet. For some reason I said, yes, I will go to your home, not knowing what to expect. Don't ask me why

I decided to go, I really don't know. Apparently, God had something in His plan for both of us.

After arriving to his home, I noticed his parents were there and I felt a little more comfortable. As we both went inside, he asked if I would have a seat in the living room and he would be right back. His Mother was in the kitchen at the time and heard us come in, but she didn't know who he had with him. He went into the kitchen and said to his mother, "I want you to meet someone that I invited to Church with me." Of course, she was very skeptical about him bringing this girl home...someone she had never met. I could tell she was very uncomfortable with this and didn't like it at all.

After meeting his mother, I continued to sit on the sofa. He went to his room stating he would be right back. Remember, this was my first time being invited anywhere with him and my first time in his home. I was on the sofa for a while not knowing he was in his room having a conversation with God about me.

As he tells the story, he heard God's voice say Angela is your wife! He said it startled him and he heard it again. Angela is your wife! He went on to say in his conversation with God that he knew a girl named Angela that he grew up with and attended church with many years ago. Could that be the one He was talking about? Then the voice of God made it clear, No! She is sitting right there on the sofa! He couldn't believe I was the Angela God was referring to. How could it be? We had not known each other long at all; I just received the Lord as my Savior, and this was my first time going anywhere with him and being in his home. How could this be? You talk about a supernatural joining; this would be it!

Once he got himself together and came out of his room to where I was, he just stood there for a moment. I asked was everything okay. Then he said, I'll be right back again. Okay! I really wandered what was going on with him. Did I make a mistake by coming to a person's home I really didn't know that well? I sat there by myself in a home I wasn't familiar with, looking around, thinking what have I gotten myself into?

Finally, he came back out of the room, but he never sat down. He gave me this look like... "I'm about to say something and I don't know why I'm even asking her this." The next thing that came out of his mouth was very unexpected and frightening. He asked me if I would marry him? Silence! Silence! Silence! That's the only way I can explain it. I didn't see that coming or knew how to respond at that moment.

As I sat there, frozen, wondering, "why is he asking me this and why now?" Something was telling me to get up, run out of there and find my way home; but something else was telling me, this is right. This was my time of decision. What answer would he receive from me? All of a sudden, I felt this peace come over me like I never felt before. It was such a calm in my frozen state. I looked to the left and then to the right, as in slow motion, with tears flowing from my eyes. The words that came out of my mouth was Yes! I will marry you! From that point on, I really can't explain what I was going through or why I said Yes! All I know is this had to be a supernatural matrimony of joining by God's order.

Once the question was asked, I accepted the proposal. The next thing was to inform our parents of our decision to get married. We both were still very young and living with our parents at the time. Before I left, we decided to share the news with his mother. After telling her, you would have thought she was slapped by the news. She said to my husband to be, "You are too young for marriage, and you just met this girl."

Next, it was my mother's turn to get the exciting news. You see, I had just graduated from high school in 1978 and I was living with my Grandfather and

Grandmother on the northside of town. I later left their home and went to live with my Great Grandmother on the eastside. In the year of 1978 of June until 1980, I lived with my mother before I got married. The time with my mother was not very long before the proposal came, and I got married. I mentioned in an earlier part of my story the reason we were apart for a time. My mother was the caretaker for my Great Grandmother on the eastside for a period of time.

I also wanted to share that when I first received Jesus as my Lord and Savior, my mother couldn't understand why I did it at such a young age. She even went to one of her friends to have them talk with me about why I would do such a thing.

Now getting back to my proposal, I knew it was time to share the news with my mother and we decided on a day to do it together. She knew I had not known this guy for long and that I had not spent much time with him at all; but she did not question me about it. With my new life in Christ, she knew I was different than the person that came to live with her at first, and she would watch me closely.

When we approached her to give her the news, of course, we both were very nervous. He went first in asking her for her daughter's hand in marriage. The expression on her face was questionable, but she did not speak against it. She thought we knew what we were doing even though we were very young. In our decision to marry, we knew he had to get to know my mother a little better.

He began coming over to visit but the only thing we would do was talk about Ministry. We would also take walks around the track which was across the street. During those times he would sing songs to me. He was a great singer and I loved to hear him sing. As God would give him songs, he would share them with me, and I will never forget them. In all of this, he would keep God first, even as we began to plan the wedding.

3

PREPARING FOR MY KING

B efore I talk about the day of the wedding, I want to share how we began preparing for it. We knew we didn't want to spend a lot for our wedding. We came up with this idea of saving our coins and putting them in a big jug to help with the cost. It was a fun idea and we were happy doing it together. It really added up quickly and helped in the planning. We got married at Mount Calvary Baptist Church in Jacksonville, Florida.

The presiding pastor was Pastor Harris at that time. This was the church my soon to be husband attended and I was okay with that. It was a very large church during that time and very active. On many occasions, I would go with him as he ministered, or I just went for a Church Service. He was very busy in the choir and leading.

We decided on the big day, which would be November 22, 1980, what a day that would be! It was a lot of fun for me getting prepared for my big day. I had to go look for my dress and, of course, my mother had to have one, as well. My Mother did not have a vehicle at the time, so her Sister offered to take us both to get our dresses. My Mother's Sister was very excited for me. I thank God for my Aunt Vivian Chisholm who has always been there for me.

4

OUR WEDDING DAY

The big day has finally come, our wedding day! We both couldn't believe how fast the year had passed. Oh! I didn't mention we had only gone out on one occasion before he proposed to me at his home. You may ask, what did you all do during that year? In our courting year we spent time together doing things like walking around the school track across the street from my home and holding hands while he would sing songs he had written. I can remember one called, "Depend On Me." It would bring me to tears every time he would sing it.

We would also attend Services at his Church, or I would support him as he ministered at other churches. Another thing we would do together was sit and watch television at my home. We both were very careful not to make covenants until we said I do. So, we did things together and in the company of others that would not stir up our emotions for each other. That was our courting time.

At that time, he did not have a car so he would ride the bus over to my home. In this part of my story, I want to mention there was no physical attraction for my husband to be, at all. It was a set-up from God, and I don't regret it at all!

Back to the wedding day, as we prepared making sure everything was in order and everyone in place, it seemed like time flew by. We would begin the wedding at 3:00p.m. that Saturday, November 22, 1980. After arriving to the church, my attendant took me to my waiting area in preparation for our ceremony. Before my father marched me down the aisle, many thoughts would begin to enter my mind. Thoughts like, I would not be single anymore and I would be leaving my mother's home. Those emotions of uneasiness along with many others tried to set in, but I accepted that this is it! I'm here now! This is the moment of truth!

As the wedding proceeded and it was time for me to line up behind the doors to enter, my father held on to me with clamped arms. The music began playing, "Here Comes The Bride,"... I held on as tight as I could in an effort not to buckle under the nervousness I was experiencing as I walked towards the front where my husband to be was waiting. As I marched down the aisle all eyes were on me.

As I was walking down the aisle, there singing, was a psalmist by the name of Paul Baskin. With every step I took, suddenly, the Psalmist began to prophesy over me. God was giving him a word about me to my future husband and who I was to him - if that makes sense! We both began to sob in tears as the word was coming forth. I believe God was confirming the joining of our union and that He had brought us together. What a day that was! I can truly say, it all came together.

Even though we had to fund most of the wedding ourselves with the saving of our coins, it was beautiful, nevertheless. The theme colors for my wedding were pastels and although it was in November, it turned out well. It was a joy to see so many family members attend our wedding. They were very supportive and was cheering us on. Many of those family members are in heaven now, but that day all in all was a grand day!

5

THE DAY AFTER THE WEDDING

After all the celebration of the wedding day, as we left the church, we entered the vehicle to drive off. We both were in amazement of what had just happened. We are married now, and we both are stepping into our new chapter of life together. No more single living, no more I, but us. After leaving the church, our driver took us to our hotel where we would stay for a few nights. You say, only a few nights? You see, my new husband had to go back to work on that Monday, so that meant we didn't have a honeymoon. From the hotel we went to live with his parents for a while until we found a home of our own.

6

THE JOURNEY BEGINS

(BIBLE COLLEGE, HOLDING DOWN A JOB AND NEWLY MARRIED)

While attending Bible College my husband was also holding down a full-time job at the Prudential Insurance Company in downtown Jacksonville. His job required him to be there very early and sometimes sleep would escape him, but he pushed. There were times that we did not see each other much during the weekdays because of his schedule of working fulltime in the day and Bible College at night. We tried to make it up on the weekends by spending time together.

During this time, we were newly married, so he was juggling Bible College, a full-time job, and a new wife. Our Saturdays and Sundays were a blur most of the time because they were already scheduled. As the days went by and the loneliness began to set in, I said to him, "I don't want to be selfish, but I don't want to be lonely either." I had to get myself together because it was agreed upon for him to go to Bible College during that time, even though I knew we were just married. I was going through newlywed anxieties of being by myself. My husband said to me, because of our decision to allow him to attend Bible College, it would benefit us both in our future together. It would make him a better man and I wouldn't regret it. That was his promise to me! I can truly say, it was worth the sacrifice.

In my settling, I decided to take on a part-time job at Winn Dixie Food Store as a cashier closer. That would occupy some of my time instead of just waiting for my husband at home. Things got better for me as time went by. He would come home at times and share many wonderful encounters they experienced in class. There was one he shared with me.

The professor required each student to give a lecture to the class on a particular assignment. As he described it, they would all go to the podium to address the class. He then said that the presence of God began to get thicker and thicker in the classroom. He said it got to the point that it was very hard to stand up because the Glory of the Lord had filled the room. He continued to say he started towards the wall and felt like he was pinned up against it and couldn't move because of the Glory of God's Presence. He said it lasted for a while as though they were captive by it. He couldn't wait to get home and share that with me.

He said he almost wanted to come get me, so I could experience it. They were allowed to bring someone to the class at least two times in a semester. He was so hyped up from this experience that it was hard for him to sleep that night knowing he had to be to work early the next day. He knew he had to count the cost. To him, it was worth it! That year he graduated salutatorian of his graduating class!

Life After Graduation...

After Bible College my husband would begin to take on many ministry assignments. At that time, there was no title attached to his name. He just wanted to be an extension of God's hands.

He was fresh out of Bible College and because I signed on to be one with him, we did it together. Let me give a backstory: My husband's early life desire was to be used by God. He would always tell the story of how he ran strong and hard for the devil in his BC days. For those who don't know, that means before he received Jesus.

When he got tired of running for the devil, he knew it was time to get his life right with the Lord. He would tell the story of how he was in high school running with the guys, being somewhat of the leader, girls would follow. He was very popular in school and graduated with high academics.

In one of his excursions, he planned a beach party, but something got hold of him and the plans changed. The next day when he went back to school, he was a different person. He explained to the guys that there would be no beach party. He went on to say, I have changed partners. What he meant was that he wasn't the same person he was yesterday. He told them; I have given my life to the Lord! Of course, the guys didn't understand but they couldn't stop him from stepping into his new life in Christ.

Instead of hanging out with the guys, he began to study his Bible and get acquainted with his new life decision. He eventually found out that a family member, for many years, was praying for him to turn his life around. Because he confided in that person, they were able to help him along the way in his daily walk in Christ.

He Wanted More...

As time went on and he wanted to learn more, one of his nieces handed him a mini book on being baptized in the Holy Spirit and speaking in tongues. That opened a whole new world for him. After immersing himself in that little book things began to happen on the inside of him. He then locked himself up in a room and asked the Lord to fill him with the evidence of speaking in his prayer language.

During that time, he was living at home with his parents. His mother heard a ruckus when he began to experience that wonderful language. She thought he and his brother were fighting, as he explained it. She was so curious until she went close to the door to hear him speaking in his heavenly language. When he came out, she looked at him as though something was wrong with him. I forgot to mention, there was a time during all this new experience that he asked the Lord to let him feel His presence strongly, as in a touch. He said the sensation he felt was so powerful that it pushed him on his bed. So, he said, do it again! Do it again! That's another reason his mother was so curious with all the noise.

From that point on the more he spent time in God's presence praying in his heavenly language, the more he wanted to! That led him into locking himself in his room for days. He only came out for school and supper at times.

He had other friends in the neighborhood that would ask if he wanted to play basketball but that wasn't his priority anymore. This is when he gave God his YES! He went on to say, that his brother noticed the change in his life, but wondered if it was real. He challenged him to see if he had really changed. With him not responding as he would have before, his brother, knew it was real. This convicted the brother and eventually he received the Lord. My husband finished high school and that was just the beginning of what God had planned for the rest of his life. Let's go back to fresh out of Bible college.

Out of the Starting Gate...

From here many opportunities opened for ministry. They were not all from behind a pulpit, but it was ministry, nevertheless. I can recall one assignment we had through one of the ministerial networks here in the city.

You could call them, and they would send you out on ministry assignments, as people needed prayer and other assistance. Depending on what area you were in, sometimes, you may be let inside their home.

As I remember two of the cases, we were sent to an elderly woman's home that could not see. She was totally blind! We took on the assignment to go to her home and she allowed us to come in. We could see as she opened the door that she was blind. We proceeded to go in and introduce ourselves and we began to minister to her. We shared the Word of God with her and began to do as Jesus did for those that needed sight. This is the part where my husband took the Bible literally. Remember when Jesus took the spittle and put it on the eyes of the blind man? You see where I'm going with this? Jesus did say to do as He did! So, he did! What do you think happened? All I can do is give you the praise report from the woman.

She said, that's a pretty dress you have on and begin to tell me about the colors in it! She continued to say I can see teeth and you have a gap. "I replied, Yes Ma'am." Of course, I wasn't offended. I was rejoicing that she could see! We all began to rejoice in the Lord! Giving God the Glory!

The Second Assignment

This prayer request was from a mother who was asking for prayer for her daughter. When he arrived at the door, she and the rest of the family allowed him in. After praying with the mother, my husband asked if the daughter was there. She replied yes and he asked if she would come in so he could pray for her, as well. He did not realize the totality of her ailment until he actually saw with his own eyes. He was astonished! When he saw the withered hand, he started thinking, this is at another level of faith.

He gathered himself and remembered if Jesus opened the eyes of the blind, could He not straighten out a withered hand? As he continued to pray for the daughter, God began to move on her. Little by little the young girl's arm was straightened and her hand became normal. How great is our God!! Everyone was in amazement at what God had done. These were just a few stories of the early assignments given as we continued our journey in ministry. "You never know where your (YES) will take you."

7

SEE HIS GLORY CRUSADES

In 1980 my husband and I started out doing what we called, "See His Glory Crusades." God would use my husband in a mighty way in the gift of healing. From there, many opportunities of travel opened the doors for ministry.

I can recall many miraculous healings taking place during the crusades. It was so wonderful watching the smiles on faces of people as the power of God moved through their bodies.

We saw people close to death revived. My husband would always share how God used him in nine different cases to speak life back into bodies that had already died. We witnessed limbs growing back, the blind eyes opened, recreation of bones and many other miraculous healings.

There were times people would say to him they saw very tall angels assisting him as he would lay hands on the sick. Some would say they saw fire in his hands or a gold like glow around him. They didn't know what to call it by what they saw, but there was no doubt that God's glory was being revealed.

I remember sitting in one of his meetings in the earlier years and as he began to minister, my hands began to burn like fire. Of course, I wondered, what is this? During this season we were newly married, but our heart was to do God's will which only brought us closer together as one.

My husband was already in ministry when we met so I became his Ruth as he continued his journey in ministry. I can truly say he didn't miss a beat, it only picked up from there.

The Crusades continued for some years before my husband decided to attend Bible College.

Bible College Years

That's a testimony within itself. My husband had a desire to go to Bible College but didn't have the resources to do so. He took his request before God in prayer about attending school. He received a call from out of nowhere asking if he was desiring to go to Bible College. The person on the phone said to him God told them in their prayer time to call this young man and pay for his tuition, so that part was taken care of and then he needed books for his classes. By faith he continued to trust God for his books. As he attended his classes, someone came up to him and asked if he had his books and he replied, "not yet." The person said, in my prayer time God spoke to me about purchasing your books. He knew without a doubt it was God's will for him attend Bible College because everything he asked God for was being taken care of.

On one of his class nights someone came to him and said can you come to my vehicle; I have something for you. They opened the trunk and there were new clothes. New trousers, shirts, and ties.

Matthew 6:25 Therefore I say unto you, take no thought for your life, what ye shall eat, or what ye shall drink; nor yet for your body, what ye shall put on. Is the life more than meat, and the body than raiment?

God will give you over and above what you ask Him for!

8

ST. GEORGE, GEORGIA

We were called to a small town about 40 miles from Jacksonville called St. George, Georgia. I don't remember the population but there were not many people and the town had only one traffic light at the time.

The journey began when two of my husband's Bible College classmates, Rocky and Paula, who were married, asked if we would consider going to St. George to do some meetings in their home. They forgot to tell us one thing about the area which was they didn't welcome people of color. As a matter of fact, we were told people of color were used for sporting. Yes! You heard me right, sporting, as in hunting you down to kill you! You would have thought my husband would say, no thanks, I'll pass but you've got to understand, he was different when it came to Kingdom business. He would let nothing stand in the way of his assignment, so he accepted the meetings. They started off small with most of their family and they began to slowly invite others in that had no problem with the color of our skin. That went on for a while.

We began traveling weekly from Jacksonville to St. George. There were times I couldn't make it with my husband, and I was very concerned about him being on those dark roads by himself at night. We became close friends with Rocky and Paula. By us becoming close friends of the family, we would plan time with them at our leisure. We never had problems in our friendship because of the color of our skin. We saw each other as sisters and brothers in the Lord. They had a big garden, and we would go there to pick berries and other vegetables at times just to fellowship with them. They were more like country folk and we were ok with that. The meetings begin to grow with more in attendance for a season. During one of the meetings the couple asked if we would stay over for a while so they could talk with us. In their area just down the road was a section called, the

Quarters. Yes! Again, you heard me right, the Quarters.

You may ask, what are the Quarters? Well, it was an area where real slaves used to live. Real slaves! Apparently, after they died, their generation of people began living in those quarters. My husband asked if they would drive him through it so he could see for himself. They did and we went to see that it was no fairytale, it did exist. The next question they asked was if we would begin ministering to those people, because we would have a better chance going in there than they would. You see their hearts were right, but their skin color was wrong. They wouldn't be received even though they lived in that area. So, of course, we took the challenge.

Remember what I said earlier in this journey to St. George, GA, our kind was not welcomed in the area. We began scheduling our days to visit the Quarters. We started by going to the homes to get to know the people. We let them know who we were and why we were there. You wouldn't believe how poor the image of the people was. It was like they were still under a master's thumb. This was in the early 80's. It was very sad to see, but we had to keep our composure. What they considered as home was unbelievable, as their floors were made of dirt and their roofs of tin.

We had to look pass what we saw and continue to minister to her. We got a chance to meet more people in the Quarters and to get acquainted with the area. They also had a building they considered a club or hang out and it was also run down. After getting the opportunity to talk to some of the people my husband and I begin to drive around to see if there was a church building there. We were told there used to be a Pastor that came monthly many years ago but that stopped, so, they did not have a pastor. We finally came across what they called the church building. It was unfinished with no restroom, no windows, a rundown piano, and dirty pews. What a sight to see!

It looked like someone had a vision for it but never completed it. As we were leaving the Quarters, we got a chance to speak with a few more people. They asked, "why are you here?" My husband replied, "I am your Pastor, and you will be seeing more of me soon." I said, "well ok!" You know we had a lot to discuss when we returned home. That was a lot to take in at once. We had never seen anything like that; realizing we were living in the 80's, but it was like living back in time.

We kept our word to the people and began going from house to house at first before we started ministering in the unfinished church. You must know we were not there for the money, because they had none to give. We were doing the work of the ministry; going out into all the world, as we are told to do in God's Word. We went to share the love of Jesus and to give back as God prospered us. We loaded up our little Toyota Nova, the car we had at the time, with blankets, clothes, shoes and whatever we thought they needed. Both of us cleaned out our closets to bless those people and we didn't give them our worse stuff. We gave them our best! The next opportunity we had to go to the Quarters, we drove in, parked the car, and allowed the people to come get whatever they wanted. They couldn't believe it and they were very thankful. Some of them had a problem receiving because of their self-image. We saw one man come to the car with his head down and he never looked up to make eye contact, as if he was ashamed. It really hurt to see that, but to God be the glory!

I can't help but tear up as I am recalling this journey in the Quarters. Knowing that there are still people who are afraid to leave their past to get to their future. As we continued to minister in the Quarters, there were salvations of those who were not intimidated by the outsiders coming in to take over. One person even brought his dog in the Service. How bold can you get? They tried to intimidate us, but we stood our ground.

For one of our arrivals back to the church on a Sunday morning someone wanted to welcome us with a burning cross; but that didn't work either! When God calls you, you must know, that you know, that you know, you were called!

9

BREAD OF LIFE RESTORATION CENTER

(HOPE FOR ALL PEOPLE)

I n our earlier years of ministry before pastoring, God graced us to start a deliverance ministry called, "Bread of Life Restoration Center Of Hope For All People." The restoration center was set up for the purpose of helping people who needed to be freed from all types of addictions that was beyond their ability to handle.

There were times when we were asked by other pastors if we would counsel their members as they would send them to us. My husband and I spent many hours with people, watching God as He would free them up. It wasn't anything we were doing ourselves, but it was by God's hands. We availed ourselves to be used by Him, so we took on the assignment for that time.

It was difficult for us at times as we watched deliverances take place in the lives of people. They would need to continue feeding on God's Word to keep themselves free, but some did not have that knowledge when they returned to their churches. We just wanted to help people!

In the ministry of deliverance, you must truly know who you are in Christ Jesus. This was another level of Ministry.

"How God anointed Jesus of Nazareth with the Holy Ghost and with power: who went about doing good and healing all that were oppressed of the devil: for God was with Him". (Acts 10:38)

"The Spirit of the Lord is upon me, because He hath anointed Me to preach the gospel to the poor; He hath sent me to heal the brokenhearted, to preach deliverance to the captives, and recovering of sight to the blind, to set at liberty them that are bruised." (Luke 4:18)

"And when He had called unto Him, He gave them power against unclean spirits, to cast them out, and to

heal all manner of sickness and all manner of disease."
(Matthew 10:1)

10

ALONG THE WAY

W here do I start on our journey of travels in ministry? We traveled many places. Our home became a big closet many days. We would pack one suitcase, return home, and repack for the next assignment. The calling on my husband's life and God's way of using him in the Apostolic and Prophetic anointing, produced a demand on his schedule to minister abroad. Those travels took us near and far, wherever the opportunity arose.

He used to tell the story of how he desired to be able to one day get on an airplane and fly to many places around the world. Some of the places were in the states and some were out of the country. Back in those days we were allowed to walk directly to the gates and watch the planes take off. He decided to go to the airport on a particular day and watch the planes take off. He said to the Lord, "I want to be able to fly around the world one day." It wasn't long after that when he received a call from Paris, France. God heard his heart's desire and things took off from there. We began traveling to Paris sometimes twice a year and many years to come. From there the invitation to India opened for Missions and it became an annual event. God had begun to open the world up to us. What a mighty God we serve! London England was another great assignment as well as the Bahamas. The experiences overall were life changing and I will never forget them.

There were many other assignments scheduled such as Africa, Australia, and others but for some reason the schedule changed. It wasn't about us. All we desired was to see change happen in the lives of people who needed a Savior, and we were vessels used by God (His Disciples).

To God be the Glory!

> "And He said unto them, Go ye into all the world, and
> preach the gospel to every creature. He that believeth
> and is baptized shall be saved; but he that believeth not
> shall be damned." (Mark 16:15-16)

11

GOD GAVE THE PUSH

The year was 1989 when we decided to come off the road and settle down to see what direction God would give us next pertaining to our lives. My husband decided that for a season we would continue our feeding at a church of a pastor he knew on the northside of town. His plan was to attend services and to be fed the Word, sit in the back, and not be bothered by anyone, to come in and get out quickly. Many people knew we had just come off the road and wondered why we were at their church. Some were very insecure because they knew we could be pastoring elsewhere and wanted to know, why are the Coleman's here?

At first, things were flowing very well then, the day came when the pastor pulled us aside after one of the Services to ask if we would help run their Tape Ministry. Of course, we accepted the assignment. Before we knew it, the next thing we were asked was to be part of the leadership group. That was very interesting to say the least. We began to attend the leadership meetings, which didn't last long for us. You ask, why? It was because we couldn't stomach the way the other leaders were treating the pastor. We had never experienced anything like that when it came to disrespecting your leadership.

My husband eventually pulled the Pastor aside to inform him our assignment was done. He was very saddened to receive the news, but he understood. We both knew it was time to get before God again for our next assignment orders. We were at our home and the Lord prompted me to go aside to pray. I went in my back room and began to cry out to God on behalf of my husband. He was thinking that my crying was because of something I was going through, until it became clear that it was about him knowing God's direction for his life. The only way to explain what was happening with me is to compare it with delivering a child. It felt as if I was pushing out a baby! That is called travailing. It means to engage in painful or laborious effort. After much travailing, the words came forth repeatedly, "show him Lord, show him Lord, show him Lord." Something began to happen to him in that moment. He heard the clarion call to pastor God's people. He described it as if God began to pour oil from his head to his feet. That's how the mantle of pastoring started.

12

BOARD MEMBERS GONE BAD

This chapter starts off in an interesting way. The mantle of pastoring was now upon my husband's life, as he had accepted the next assignment. The questions to answer would be, "where to go, when to begin and how?" As time went by and there were opportunities for my husband to minister in other churches, he received a call from a pastor in the city to come in. All went well and the people received him kindly. They didn't know the Pastor was planning to resign from the Church and was recruiting someone to take his place.

The Pastor would often have staff meetings with his people and at a particular meeting he invited us to come in. We had no idea why he would invite perfect strangers, but my husband accepted. Because we did not know the Pastor that well, nor his people, we didn't realize what would take place in the board meeting that evening. The tensions got so heated that they almost "threw hands" to fight one another. Yes! In the Church! With the Pastor!

Of course, we looked at each other in disbelief that this was really happening. We were people of peace and we politely brought order back to the table. That would be the last meeting we would attend. Lo and behold, the Pastor contacted my husband again to meet with him on a certain matter. Can you guess what it was? Yes! He was asked to take over the pastorate of the Church. Now we understood why we were invited to the meeting.

My husband was told by the former Pastor that he wanted to resume his pastoral duties out of the country. We found out that his words were a total lie. He never left this soil. He just wanted a way out of that church and away from those rebellious people. We saw this as an opportunity to begin the pastoral assignment. You see, my husband always loved a challenge! Nothing was too big in his eyes to handle because he knew God was in control. That was the start of our lives in the pastoral office; in what we call our first Church!

The congregation didn't have a clue that their Pastor was in route of departing. This was devastating news for some, but they eventually got over it. Now here come the new Pastors! The journey starts out with what we thought would be a good group of people to shepherd, but we had another thing coming that we didn't see. The Board! It consisted of two married couples that had been friends for years. They were very prominent people and very influential. After getting to know them, that was far from what we experienced having them close to us, as they continued to be on the board of the church.

They thought being up under the former Pastor and having special privileges, as in running things, would carry over to the newbies, Us. But they had another thing coming! A new sheriff had taken over. First, it started with the church secretary. She thought she would continue her role with the new pastors coming in. We decided to interview her to see if she would work out. After the interview we wondered how in the world did he have her as a secretary? We believed it was for other reasons.

My husband asked her to take a letter to type. We found out that she had a problem with very simple spelling, and she failed in every assignment we gave her. That didn't go across well with her to know that she wasn't working out. We didn't ask her to leave the Church, but her secretarial duties were over. She also had given some wood to the Church many years ago and after being released from the office, she asked, to get her wood back. We had no idea what she was talking about.

We found out the wood she donated to the Church was not in any condition to be used and termites had eaten it up. That was the first situation we had to deal with. Secondly, the Drummer in the Church, this young man had an addiction to crack cocaine. He was paid weekly by the Church to finance his habit. We delicately pulled him aside and tried to bring restoration to him, but he also refused our help and wanted to leave because he would no longer receive money to pay for his habit. Joy of Joys! We couldn't in good conscious continue to pay him knowing how he would use the money.

We continued to encourage one another knowing this was just the start of the assignment. As time went by, we began to meet with the Board on a regular basis and things seemed pretty normal.

One of the couples on the Board invited us over to their home to get to know us better. They fed us a good meal, one of my favorites, fish and grits, and I tell you it was very good! They seemed well-balanced at first until time went on. Then I got a better understanding of what Jesus went through with Judas! We should have known after a good meal together what would happen. There was another couple there on the Board who would smile in your face and hide their hands behind their back. You see, they both were working together all the time. It reminds me of an old song from years ago: The lyrics were very true..." They smilin' in your face only to take your place, Back Stabbers!" Those words panned out to be true.

Now getting back to the first couple that fed us the good meal of fish and grits, I will call them the Jones.' The husband of the Jones' would begin to show his real self as time went on. We didn't realize that he had a key to the Pastor's office and would go through the mail as he wished. My husband decided to arrive to the office early and caught him scrouging through the mail and asked what he was doing and why did he have a key to the office? He went on to say that the last Pastor approved of it, but he had no explanation of why he was in the Pastor's office going through the mail. That was Strike one!

The next bold thing he did was to ask my husband to

stop preaching on certain subjects and threatened if he didn't that, he would stop paying his tithe. Oh boy, Strike two! My husband politely asked him to come to the office on tomorrow to have a talk. When he arrived, my husband called him into the office and asked him to have a seat. Then, my husband began to write on a piece of paper, not lifting his head, while the man quietly sat in front of him, until he was finished. After sitting a while, he got impatient and asked, what are you writing? My husband proceeded to answer, "Your resignation from the Board and the Church, if necessary." Do you recall Jesus' writing in the sand? That's what comes to mind. He went on to say, "You or no one else will never bribe, insult or intimidate me by pulling your tithe from the Church. You will never buy me out! You may have gotten away with a lot of things with the old Pastor, but I'm not the one." He also said to him, "I will get a better return by flushing your tithe down the toilet."

Can you imagine what happened after that meeting? He didn't leave the office a happy camper. But there again, it didn't matter. There was no compromising on this new assignment. Now that stirred up some things with both couples on the Board and a few others they had influence with in the Church. They didn't leave the Church at that point, but, yes, they did want to take it over. They knew they had to do something about the new Pastor coming in the Church and changing things.

Now let's go back to the couple who I will call, the Browns'. The husband of the Browns' decided one Sunday morning during the Service that he would stay outside and pass out flyers against us as the people were coming into the Church. We continued to have Service not knowing what was going on outside. As my husband was ministering, one young lady brought him a flyer. I can't recall what it said, but it wasn't good. All I knew is they wanted us out. My husband took the flyer and held it up to the congregation and said, "You all see this piece of paper? It is trash! And that's where it belongs...in the trash!" Some of them began to see that he was not easily moved by the foolishness but would continue to preach God's Word. They tried this and that, until the next thing. We knew God had sent us to that Church to rescue some and that's what happened.

The other thing we had to correct was the way the people were praying. It was totally off! They needed much structure and a new way of feeding. Some accepted and some refused because they were used to the old way of thinking and doing things. We had to reassign strong intercessors over the Church with our spirit.

We also knew the old Board was out and would be revamped. Many changes had to take place to have a peaceful flow. That meant every ministry in the Church had to be restructured. Just like we do a house cleaning, there had to be a Church cleaning. The purpose is to be changed to light because there was much darkness inside the church and the people. That's why we had a spiritual fight on our hands. But God prevailed!

Lastly, this was the Whammy! Back to the Jones'. This time, the wife was in charge. She was a very influential woman in the city and was well off financially. Between both couples, they were all well off. When we would share this story, people thought we were making it up, but this really happened. Mrs. Jones, the wife, felt like they had enough with the new Pastors. She decided to plan her hit on my husband and those close to him. Her plan was to hire a hit man and it didn't matter the cost and she made sure he was skilled in using a machete. That's how she wanted to take my husband out, while he was preaching. The way he found out was someone called the church office.

He picked up the phone to hear someone say: "Do you value your life?" As he began to speak, they abruptly told him to be quiet and listen. They said, "One of your members paid a hit man to come to your Church and take you out." By this time there was a new secretary in the Church, Vanilla Deas (aka – Vanilla Pittman) who is now the Senior Associate Pastor of Voice of Joy Word Ministries, International. She also heard the threat and was very concerned. My husband told her not to let me know about the threat, but I eventually found out. We were told the man could come at any time during our Services but that didn't stop us from doing the will of God. We prayed more and continued the assignment. I know you're asking; did he finally show up? Not at all, but she did pay someone to carry it out. She was forgiven for that one, but the kicker was that she didn't give up!

She wanted to give it one more try, so she went to a mental hospital and released a patient and gave them a picture of my husband to go and take him out at the Church. This is real stuff! And it really happened. I was there, and so was God!

I didn't find out about this, what I referred to as a "confused woman" at first. She had apparently gone to the Church the day before to intimidate my husband at the Church office. Of course, she was not in her right mind, and she should have never been released out of the mental hospital or driving anybody's car. Mrs. Jones got her out for one last assignment. This lady was given a car to drive, and she had a picture of her parents in the backseat that she would talk to before she would do her craziness. Her parents were both dead! You see how desperate some people are when they're listening to the devil? In this instance I'm speaking of Mrs. Jones. They wanted us to leave the Church so bad that they would do anything no matter the cost. On the next day, my husband picked me up from work he told me what had happened with this lady. Being the person I am, I said to my husband, "Take me by the office today so I can see this person you're talking about."

So, he did, and I was not ready for what I would encounter that day. It was unreal but it happened! As we pulled up in front of the building, which at that time was a store front building, we sat there for a moment to see if she would return. Lo and behold, here she comes.

Something rose on the inside of me so strongly, I began to speak in tongues, aiming my prayer directly at her. As I jumped out of my car to head towards her, she quickly put her foot on the gas and sped off from the parking lot. We were thinking she had left, never to return, but that was not the case. Before we knew it, here she comes again! This time she stopped near the end of the street of the parking lot. At that moment, one of our members pulled up and parked next to our vehicle, right in front of the entrance to the Church. The member didn't know what was going on when he got out of his car to talk with us. We quickly jumped out of our vehicle to let him know what was going on with her.

I didn't mention that I had one of our babies in my arms as we were headed towards the entrance door of the Church. All of a sudden, we noticed a raring up of a motor from the car heading our way. This lady put the car in gear, coming at a fast speed directly where we were standing. My husband pushed me away and the member so we wouldn't get hit by this car. To protect us from the woman, my husband took an iron pole and would have used it as a javelin to stop her. He would have used whatever was necessary to stop her! She was out of her mind and Mrs. Jones knew it. The only thing on this woman's mind was to take out the person that was on the picture given to her. You're probably wondering by now, what happened to the woman. I'm about to tell you! Remember what I told you at the start of the fiasco. Mrs. Jones released this mental patient out of the hospital, rented her a car, gave her my husband's picture, and told her he was trying to take her husband's church. We called 911 and the police arrived eventually. Here's what happened: We told him what had happened, and that this lady was let out of a mental hospital by one of the board members of the Church. He couldn't believe someone would do such a thing. This part is funny now, but not funny, then!

The policeman looked at the lady and said, "I remember you!" His next words were, "Who let you out?" Then, she held a picture up to him and said, "This man is trying to take my husband's Church!" If they didn't know before, they knew right then that she had mental issues. They called in a female officer and booked her. The old board member was never charged for releasing her from the mental hospital, but I can tell you, her conscious ate her up from that day on for the rest of her life knowing what she had done.

We had to forgive her and that's exactly what we did. The next time we saw Mrs. Jones was at a restaurant buffet many, many years later. My husband was right next to her getting his food and didn't have any ill feelings toward her. It's like he didn't recall any of the things she had done. That's real love!

13

I DIDN'T SEE THIS COMING

Because my husband and I were so intertwined as one, we would spend most of our time and days together bouncing ideas off each other for the next assignment to come. His normal schedule would be to get up very early in the mornings between 3:00a.m. – 4:00a.m. Because he lived a life of prayer, that was his morning regimen. Sometimes he would pray at home, or he would go to the church to the Prayer Wall, but he wouldn't allow anything to get in the way of that time with God. He took his prayer time seriously.

On one of those particular days, everything seemed normal as we went about our daily schedules, or so I thought. On May 10, 2019, around 7:00p.m., we were both sitting in our family room holding a normal conversation as we would sometimes. When my husband asked to excuse himself for a moment and he would soon return. Moments before, we were laughing and joking with one another before he excused himself. After moments of waiting, I decided to go check on him in our back-room area. As I noticed, he was getting ready to return from that area. As he stood up from his sitting position, I watched him just fall to the floor. I quickly ran towards him to see what had happened, but he didn't respond. I then begin to call out to him and started praying in the Spirit over him. At that moment, I wondered what was going on.

All of a sudden, he returned to consciousness, and I had him to sit down to figure out what just happened to him. I then asked him if he needed me to call 911. He never answered, he was just staring off. So, I took the initiative to do so anyway. Elder Selby, at that time, stopped by our home to drop off a package for Bishop. She had not planned to stay but I needed her help. She ran in as I was trying to lift him up from the floor. Believe me, it wasn't in my own strength. She watched with me as something strange began to happen with him. We watched him go into a stare as if he was focused on something that he never took his eyes off.

That's the only way I can explain it! (I was trying to see where I could help him and he was abruptly telling me to move out of the way of whatever he was seeing, as if he didn't want me to step in the path of it. I know it might sound strange but that's what happened at that moment. Because it didn't seem normal to me what happened with him falling, I went ahead and called 911 to have him checked out.

When the paramedics arrived at our home they were led to where he was sitting. One of the paramedics asked if my husband could stand up. His exact words were "Buddy, can you stand up?" He then said to the paramedic, "I need oxygen!" As he proceeded to stand on his own, he fell again! This time they tried to bring him to consciousness in the area where he was, but they couldn't, so they had to pull him into another area to begin CPR. As I stood there watching my husband's lifeless body, I felt numb. All I could do was begin to pray as I watched them take turns to get a heartbeat and continue to check his pulse.

After they worked for a while and it seemed like a long time, right there in my living area, it didn't seem real. When they couldn't get a heartbeat, they decided to take him out and continue to do CPR in the ambulance. They never rushed to leave for the hospital, as they kept working on him. (I believe when he took that second fall, he met Jesus!) The paramedics finally decided to go ahead to the hospital, and they told me where they were going, as I followed behind. I was not allowed to ride in the ambulance, so I had to drive my own vehicle.

Once we got to the hospital, I was waiting in the waiting area for a while wondering when someone would come give me information on how he was doing. It seemed like I waited forever. I finally went to the desk to ask for information about my husband and I was told they were still working on him, and someone would be out to speak with me momentarily. I waited more until I was finally called to a room with a few family members. I wasn't prepared for what I heard next! The doctor gave me that unwanted stare directly into my eyes and said, "I'm sorry, we did all we could do!!!"

At that moment, it's like I left the room, my body became like jelly. I had to catch my breath and my knees began to buckle and become lifeless. I then fell to the floor, uncontrollably done.

That is something I never want to experience again in my life! The only way I can describe it is like a part of me left. Now in having someone to comfort me, I also had to comfort our girls, Erica, and Charity, because they were so close to their father. It had only been two years since their grandmother transitioned and they were still dealing with that. To add to that, the rest of the family, the grandbabies, the church family, spiritual sons, and daughters and many more would have received this terrible news. How do you tell people your Leader has transitioned when he was just in their presence? This was a shock to all!

I thank God for our Pastors, Vanilla Pittman and Andrea Selby, who have never left my side. They encouraged me to KEEP PUSHING!

SPECIAL TESTIMONIES

The Beginning of the Battle: Standing on our Faith (Erica's Story)

At the age of six, our daughter, Erica was scheduled for a regular appointment with the Pediatrician. We were told there were some deficiencies in her body that would need serious attention. Of course, it wasn't something that was a quick fix. We were told to get her to the hospital for further observation.

As the years went by, my husband and I watched her very closely and cared for her as best we knew how. We were both very young and had been married for only four years when we had Erica. In my lifetime I've seen many marriages that didn't make it where a sickly child was involved. I thank God I had a God-fearing man, my husband who was also a caretaker, in my life.

We were both working outside the home at that time, so we had to trust others to care for our child. My Mother was available to care for Erica for a while. The only downside was that she lived on the other side of town, but we were grateful she was available. Because of the deficiencies in our child's body, anyone caring for her had to be trained when she was in a crisis. Over the years there were many people God sent to be a help.

As Erica grew, she had to learn what was going on in her body and how to counteract it. In the case of a crisis, there was much work for us all, sometimes little or no sleep. It got to the point that my husband and I said to God, "If you can't keep her, she can't be kept!"

As our daily lives went on, I can remember when Erica was nine years old and on a Sunday morning we were preparing to go to church as we regularly did. Erica was looking a little peaked, but we didn't think it was serious enough to keep her home. After the Sunday Service was over, we decided to go to my husband's parent's home which was near the Church. They were both home at the time.

Special Testimonies

When we went in and got settled, Erica told her father she needed to use the bathroom which was different on that day because we were keeping a close watch over her. Only a few minutes had past when we heard a blood curdling scream come from the bathroom. Her father ran in just in time to catch her as she was falling on the floor. He picked up her lifeless body and put her on his parents' bed checking for a pulse. We both were in shock and felt paralyzed at that moment. We couldn't even remember the number to call for Emergency Assistance! (911) We both were baffled, asking what is the number? It was that real.

We were still working on our daughter to get breath, but nothing was happening; at that moment we were not God's "super parents." This was our child and none of what was happening made sense. We continued to do CPR as we were waiting on the ambulance to arrive to his parents' home. During all of this, his parents couldn't even come into their room to see their lifeless grandchild on the bed.

The ambulance finally arrived. It seemed like it took forever for them to come. They, of course, asked their questions while others tried to resuscitate our daughter. From that point, everything seemed to go in slow motion. As one of the paramedics picked up our nonresponsive, daughter's body to carry her to the

69

ambulance, he had already decided to call in a DOA report on our child. He proceeded to pull a cover over her face as they were sure she was gone.

At that point, I couldn't look at my child in that state, so I told my husband I would drive behind the ambulance. He climbed into the back of the ambulance with the paramedic and our lifeless daughter's body covered from head to toe. There were no sirens or lights flashing to indicate life. During all of this, my husband was having a conversation with God as he looked at her lifeless body. In his words, as he would always share with many people, "My wife and I prayer for this child, in conception, was specific. We told God what we wanted and how we wanted her to be – gender, complexion, hair type, etc. We said we wanted a light-skinned, curly haired, baby girl and that's just what God gave us in our first child together."

I prayed for a supernatural childbirth and that's what God gave me. During labor and delivery, the doctors didn't have to give me anything. When the time came to deliver this child, they just watched us do all the work. I stood on God's Word, feeding myself every scripture on childbirth. It was truly supernatural. My friend gave me a book called, "Supernatural Childbirth." I've shared the book with many since then. There were many powerful testimonies from those who used it. I shared all that information to let you know that the life of our daughter was supernatural and that's why it didn't make sense to see her in an ambulance, lifeless.

Back to the conversation my husband was having with God, his prayer was, "Lord you gave my wife and I this child and we've prayed many things over her life. This is not the way it's supposed to happen." Then he said he heard these words, "She is a child of promise!" He heard it again, "She is a child of promise!" He said something began to rise up in him, and he said, "Yeah, she is a child of promise!" "Yeah, she is a child a promise!" He began to repeat those words over and over. The paramedic that was in the rear of the ambulance with my husband asked, "What was her name?"

He didn't quickly answer back because he wasn't going to agree with the word, "was." Out of my husband's spirit came the words, "Her name is Erica." Then he asked the paramedic to call her name, of course, he thought my husband had lost it! He said, "she's already gone, Sir." My husband asked him again to call her name. There no response for 19 minutes and 47 seconds. They had already called in a DOA. By the 3rd time the paramedic called her name, she pulled the cover down, as she grasped for air! Everything changed! They quickly turned on the lights and sirens and called the dispatcher. The paramedic began to shout, "We got life!" (The number (3) biblically represents divine wholeness, completeness, and perfection.)

It scared the paramedics. All they knew was that this child was already gone, and they had already called in a DOA. By the time they arrived at the hospital, the dispatcher couldn't believe what happened. They quickly got her in and checked her out, making sure her oxygen levels were flowing correctly. After getting her settled in and checking her out, they agreed to put her in ICU for more observation. After a period of days, she was put into a step-down unit, where she was still watched closely before being transferred to a regular hospital room.

Can somebody say, But God! My encouragement to all that will have the opportunity to read this book is to "Never give up!" It may seem like and it may look like you've lost the fight, but hold on to the finish! It's not over until God says it's over! Psalm 89:34 says, "My covenant will I not break, nor alter the thing that has gone out of my lips." Amen!

Charity's Testimony: Battle 2, Our Youngest Child (Continuing to Stand)

I'm going to start this chapter by saying, "You must stand your ground, regardless." The enemy doesn't play fair. Not only does he want to steal, kill, and destroy your life, but also the lives of your children, your seed. (John 10:10)

Charity's Story

Charity, our youngest daughter, was having a normal day at home. She and our oldest daughter, Erica, decided to clean the house. I was busy in the back area and my husband was away at the office working. Charity had taken the chore of vacuuming and Erica, dusting. They had a plan and of course, I was happy. The next thing I heard was Erica screaming at the top of voice for me to come to the room where they were cleaning.

Erica explained to me that she turned around to see the vacuum cleaner still running but no Charity. She went on to explain that she thought her sister was trying to get something from under the table but found out she was having a Grand Mal Seizure. That was the reason she was under the table and not moving, convulsing with her teeth clenched together. She was also unable to walk. I quickly called her father and he met us at the hospital; it being closer than trying to come home. As Erica and I got Charity into the vehicle, I had Erica keep her alert as we rushed to the hospital praying fast and hard that she would stay conscious. When we finally got to the hospital, they rushed her in and began to take her vital signs, mainly to her brain.

My husband and I were still young, having to stand firm in our faith. After running many tests on Charity, the doctors didn't give us any positive news about her diagnosis. They told us she would be on seizure medication for the rest of her life. They prescribed medication for her to take daily and for regular doctor visits. This meant we had to pay much money to hospitals and take time off from our jobs.

Something had to give.

We began to anoint her daily with oil [James 5:14, "Is any sick among you? Let him call for the elders of the church; and let them pray over him, anointing him with oil in the name of the Lord."] and continue keeping her covered in prayer. When we purchased the medication, we made sure we prayed over it. Every time she took the medication we said, "this is unto the day that she will no longer need it."

We would take Charity to her appointments, sometimes together and other times separately because of our schedules. Every time I would take her, I would pray under my breath and talk to God, saying to Him, "It won't be this way always." I can remember at one of her appointments, as her father was talking with the Doctor, I became full hearing the negative words come from his mouth. I left the room and went down the hallway to talk with God! I began to remind Him of the healing scriptures in His Word and the promises in His Word to us and our children. I continued to tell the devil, No! No! you can't have our children! They are a gift from God.

You see the Bible tells us in James 1:17, "Every good and perfect gift is from above, and cometh down from the Father of lights with Whom is no variableness, neither shadow of turning.

> "*Children are God's love-gift. They are heaven's generous reward.*" (Psalm 127:3 TPT)

> "*Don't you see that children are God's best gift? The fruit of the womb His generous legacy?*" (Psalm 127:3 MSG)

All I can say is God is true to His Word! Another Victory! All praises to our God! Remember, there is a God part and there is a people part to play. We administered the medication to our daughter as prescribed by the Doctors. Their prediction was that she would be on the medications for life. Our prayer was that she was "the healed" and that's what we stood on. To God be the glory!

Charity went to one of her doctor's appointments and was taken off the medication in less than a year! There were no more signs of seizures and none to return. What a day that was! Our God is Faithful!

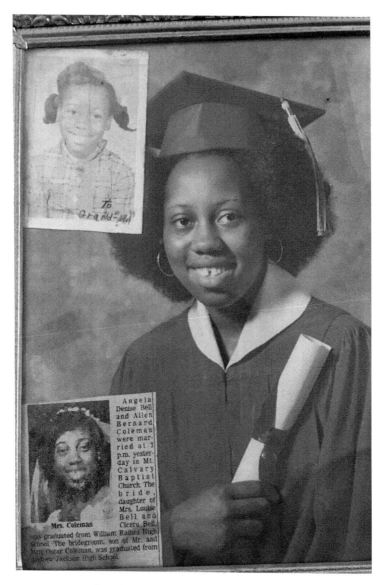

Angela Coleman, Graduation – 1978, Married – 1980

Wedding Day, November 22, 1980

Angela Coleman, (At our Church Service on Ellis Rd. with guest speaker, Pastor Rajiah of Paris, France)

Angela Coleman (At our Church on Old Kings Rd.)

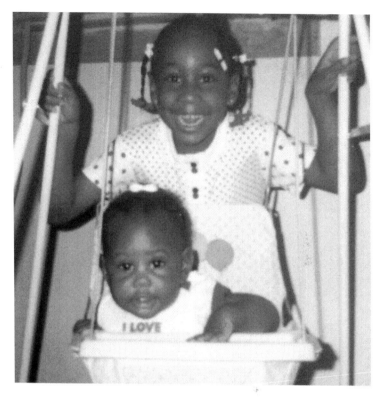

Our Girls, top – Erica, bottom – Charity

Daddy – Daughter Moment (Charity with (Father), Bishop Allen Coleman)

Left to right: Charity, Mom, Erica

Mom, Erica & Dad

Preaching in Paris, France for our friends, Pastors' Rajiah

In lobby of hotel in Paris, France

Sharing together on a Region Voice Radio Broadcast

Bishops' Appreciation Event

On Vacation in Niagara Falls, Canada

One Heart Couples Banquet

We received our Doctorate Degrees

Early years of Ministry

ABOUT THE AUTHOR

Overseer Angela Coleman is the Co-Founder and General Overseer of Voice of Joy Word Ministries, International - a Full Gospel, Interdenominational Christian Fellowship whose vision is to "empower a people to serve a powerful God." She was married to the late Bishop Allen B. Coleman for 39 years. To their union are two daughters, Erica Adam (Andrew III) and Charity Coleman; and four grandchildren - Andrew IV, Angela, Allen and Amarissa. She continues the legacy and the Kingdom work assignment of "Total Man Ministry."

For information on bulk ordering this title or for distribution
questions, contact us at:

Tall Pine Books
119 E Center Street, Suite B4A | Warsaw, Indiana 46580
www.tallpinebooks.com

Made in the USA
Columbia, SC
10 February 2022

54935957R00059